Rumi

The Persian Mystic

Frederick Hadland Davis

CONTENTS

EDITORIAL NOTE

The object of the editors of this series is a very definite one. They desire above all things that, in their humble way, these books shall be the ambassadors of goodwill and understanding between East and West, the old world of Thought, and the new of Action. In this endeavour, and in their own sphere, they are but followers of the highest example in the land. They are confident that a deeper knowledge of the great ideals and lofty philosophy of Oriental thought may help to a revival of that true spirit of Charity which neither despises nor fears the nations of another creed and colour. Finally, in thanking press and public for the very cordial reception given to the "Wisdom of the East" series, they wish to state that no pains have been spared to secure the best specialists for the treatment of the various subjects at hand.

L. CRANMER-BYNG,
S.A. KAPADIA.

4, HARCOURT BUILDINGS,
INNER TEMPLE,
LONDON.

PREFACE

I desire to thank Mr. R.A. Nicholson for his kind and generous permission to use selections from his *diwane Shams Tabraiz,* and also his publishers, the Cambridge Press. I am deeply indebted to Mr. E.H. Whinfield for allowing me to use quotations from his rendering of the *Masnavi* (Trubner's Oriental Series). I also cordially thank Mr. John Hastie for giving me permission to quote a few passages from the late Rev. Professor Hastie's "Festival of Spring" (James Maclehose & Sons, Glasgow). The poems quoted from this volume are entitled: "Thy Rose," "I saw the Winter weaving," "Love sounds the Music of the Spheres," "The Souls Love-moved," and "The Beloved All in All." All the other translations from the lyrical poetry of Jalãlu'ddîn Rûmî are by Mr. R.A. Nicholson. To these gentlemen, and to those I have left unnamed.

I tender my warmest thanks for their help, sympathy, and interest in my attempt to "popularise the wisest of the Persian Sûfis."

F. HADLAND DAVIS.

LONDON:

INTRODUCTION

I. The Origin of Sufiism

Among the Mohammedans Sûfiism, or Persian mysticism, is known as *tasawwuf.* The word Sûfi is derived from *sûf,* meaning "wool." When a littel Persian sect at he end of the eighth century A.D. broke away from the orthodox Muslim religion, and struck out on an independent path, they ignored costly robes and worldly ostentation, and clad themselves in a white wool garment. Hence they were known as "wool wearers," or Sûfis.

Prof. Edward G. Browne[1] gives four theories in regard to the origin of Sûfiism, *viz. : (1) Esoteric Doctrine of the Prophet (2) Reaction of the Aryan mind against a Semitic religion. (3) Neo-Platonist influence. (4) Independent origin.* Neither of the four theories altogether satisfies the

1. A literary History of Persia. vol. i.

learned professor, and very certain it is that the last-mentioned theory is of very little account. Prof. Browne seems in favour of a "spontaneous growth" existing in various forms, under various names throughout the civilised world; but after all this is not very tangible evidence. Moreover, we must bear in mind that the Neo-Platonist philosophers paid a visit to the Persian court in the sixth century A.D., and founded a school there in the reign of Noûshîrwãn. It is highly probable, therefore, that these seven philosophers forced to leave their homes through the tyranny of Justinian, who forbade the teaching of philosophy at Athens, should have had considerable influence upon a few of the more thoughtful Persians. We shall now find that this theory is borne out by internal evidence.

Let us briefly study the tenets of Neo-Platonism. The Neo-Platonists believed in the existent, it generated from itself. Creation was the reflection of its own Being. Nature, therefore, was permeated with God. Matter was essentially non-existent, a temporary and ever-moving shadow for the embodiment of the Divine. The Neo-Platomists believed that by ecstasy and contemplation of the All-Good, man would rise to that Source from whence he came. These points bear directly upon the Sûfi teaching. They form a broad outline of the tenets of Sûfiism. The Sûfis, from temperamental and other causes, elaborated these ideas, gave them a rich and beautiful setting, and, what is all-imoportant, built about them one of the most interesting phases of mystical poetry the world has ever known, and this particular phase may be said to date from the twelfth century A.D.

Thus, I think, it will be readily admitted that the Sûfis certainly owed something to the Neo-Platonists. The cry for the Beloved was in their hearts before the Greek philosophers came; but Neo-Platonism appealed to their Orientla minds. It was a stepping-stone across the river of their particular spiritual tendencies, and they trod thereon, and proceeded to lay down other stones across the stream. I have pointed out the similarities between this particular Greek and Persian belief.

There was, however, one very important difference. The Neo-Platonists's conception of God was purely abstract, the Sûfî's essentially personal, as far as the early Sûfîs were concerned. We shall consider other influences which were brought to bear upon Sûfîism a little later on. There is a very great difference between the early Sûfîism and the elaborate additions that followed as an evolutionary matter of course.

In brief, then, Neo-Platonism was the doctrine of Ecstasy. A quotation from the letter of Plotinus to Flaccus on Ecstasy will still further show the similarities between this Greek and Persian teaching:

"The wise man recognises the idea of the Good within him. This he develops by withdrawal into the Holy Place af his own soul. He who does not understand how the soul contains the Beautiful within itself, seeks to realise beauty without, by laborious production. His aim should rather be to concentrate and simplify, and so to expand his being; instead of going out into the Manifold, to forsake it for the One, and so to float upwards towards the Divine Fount of Being whose stream flows within him."

This is Sûfiism in prose. The Sûfis turned the same conception into *poetry*.

II. The Early Sufis

ABU HASHIM (ob.150 A.H.) was the first to bear the name of Sûfi, while Dhu'nnûnal-Misri (245 A.H.) may be said to have given Sûfiism its permanent shape. Rabi'a, of Basra, was the first woman to join the sect, and her saintliness and wise sayings have been preserved by Faridu'ddin 'Attãr. One day a great sickness fell upon Rãbi'a, and on being asked the reason for it she replied: "I dwelt upon the joys of Paradise and therefore my Beloved has chastened me." Rãbi'a did not believe in earthly marriage. Her remark on the subject is given as follows: "The bonds of wedlock have descended upon me. I am not my own, but my Lord's, and must not be unfaithful to Him." 'Attãr also informs us that when Rãbi'a was asked if she hated the devil, she replied: "My love to God leaves me no time to hate him." Rãbi'a was a woman of much independence of thought, ethical rather than metaphysical in her remarks, and strongly opposed to outward ceremonials. She is said to have died at Jerusalem, 753 A.D. It was at Ramla, in Palestine, that a Christian nobleman built a convent (*Khãnqãh*) for the Sûfis. Thus in the early days the sect defied their Prophet's condemnation of monkery by building an abode for members of the order. The Sûfis were strongly opposed to the idea of free will or distinct and self-existent personality apart from the Beloved. The orthodox Muslim's idea was precisely the reverse. The Sûfis have always made the Quran their text-book. With infinite licence they ingeniously quote therefrom, and still more ingeniously add their own explanations when necessary. No doubt there were political reasons for adopting this method of concealing heterodox ideas under the cloak of orthodoxy. We shall see, however, as the sect grew and still further broadened its views, that these clever compromises did not prevent the appearance of martyrs among their number in the future.

By the end of the second century of the Hijira the Sûfis were a much-respected religious order. In the following century Quietism had not only changed to Pantheism, but Pantheism had kindled a belief that Beloved and lover were identical. The step was inevitable and at this juncture it was that Sûfiism became essentially mystical, and it became more mystical as years advanced. About this time, viz., the beginning of the third century A.H., we come across two interesting Sûfis who seem to have been the prime movers in this new development, by name Bãyazid and Mansur al-Hallãj.

Concerning the saint Bãyazid an interesting story is told in the Fourth Book of the *Masnavi*. The saint surprised his disciples one day by saying: " Lo, I myself am God Almighty. There is no God beside me; worship me! "The disciples, thinking their Master was beside himself, told him, when the strange ecstasy had passed, what he had said.

Bãyazid promptly replied: "If I do so again straightway slay me! "His disciples accordingly sharpened their knives. Once more Bãyazid cried out: "Within my vesture is naught but God, whether you seek Him on earth or heaven." The disciples; horror-struck at his remarks, straightway plunged their knives into Bãyazid's body. But their blades were turned back against their own, throats, so that they died. He explained to the few disciples, who had not struck him, that the ecstasy he had been experiencing annihilated self, "His form is vanished, he is a mere mirror." The disciples who had struck him saw their own faces in that mirror and so wounded themselves, and not Bãyazid, whose soul had left the mirror of his body' and was one with the Beloved.

Perhaps the life of Mansur al-Hallãj is even more interesting. Whether he was a mere adventurer or genuine exponent of Sûfiism is still open to controversy among modern Sûfis. It will be perfectly safe to describe him as either a saint or a vagabond. He was possibly both extremes to suit the necessities of a very exciting and eventful career. He was born in the close of the ninth century A.D., and was said to perform many miracles, such as raising the dead to life; and drawing gold and flowers from the air. Accordimg to his own belief he could write verses equal to those of the Quran. He went one better than the "superman" theory, however, and called himself God, and his disciples after the various prophets. Akbar was called God, but deification in this case did not sound from his own trumpet; it sounded from the trumpet of an enthusiastic poet: "See Akbar and you see God." Al-Hallāj visited India for the purpose of studying magic, and there saw the celebrated Rope Trick, on that occasion performed by a woman, a point of considerable interest.[1] This mystic-adventurer wrote fortysix books, and certainly gained considerable influence over the lower classes by his many signs and wonders. He is said to have disputed the necessity of making a pilgrimage to Makkah by stating that by occult

1. "Among the Adepts and Mystics of Hindustan." The Occult Review, December, 1905.

practices it could be performed equally well in any room. On a certain occasion, however, we cannot help but admire Al-Hallãj's wit and aptitude. One day he stretched forth an empty hand and produced from the air an apple, which he asserted he had: plucked from Paradise. One of his witnesses. disputed his assertion, because this particular apple was maggot-eaten, and therefore not of Divine origin. Al-Hallãj at once replied: "It is because it hath come forth from the Mansion of Eternity to the Abode of Decay: therefore to its heart hath corruption found its way!"

Al-Hallãj, on account of his various heretical teachings, was imprisoned and subjected to all manner of cruelties. Bravely he went forth to the place of crucifixion. For four days he was nailed on a cross on both sides of the Tigris: From these tortures he was finally released. Ten years later he was executed, telling his disciples he would return to them in thirty days, and exultantly reciting poetry, he cried: "From His own cup He bade me sup, for such is hospitality!" A comment of his on

Sûfiism—a very ironical one—was: "That which is mine, for by God I never distinguished for a moment between pleasure and pain!" Yet another characteristic, saying of his was: "The way to God is two steps: one step out of this world, and one step out of the next world, and lo! you are there with the Lord!" Whatever were the faults of Al-Hallãj, and they were many, at least it may be said of him that he was a brave man. With all his fanaticism, his absurd indiscretion and love of conjuring, he left much behind of permanent value to the Sûfis. The Government, in those days, did all in its power to restrain the publicity of his books; but a light that was never for a moment set under a bushel cannot be hid; the very attempt to obliterate it is in itself the cause for a keener and more persistent search.

In the fifth century of the Hijira we may note Abu-l-Khair as the first to give Sûfiism political significance, and Imãm Ghazzãli as the first to give it a metaphysical basis. At this time we find in Sûfi books many terms borrowed from the Neo-

Platonists. Books on ethics, as well as poetry, now became impregnated with Sûfi ideas.

III. The Nature of Sufiism

> The Sûfis are folk who have preferred God to everything, so that God has preferred them to everything.—**DHU' NNUN.**[1]

IN the Islãmic faith there are eight Paradises arranged one within the other in ascending stages. The highest is called "The Garden of Eden." All are lovely gardens full of luxuriant flowers and trees, amid which gleam the domes and minarets of gorgeous palaces, rich with precious stones, where the departed are feasted and entertained by beautiful *houris*. All the Paradises are watered by rivers, such as the Kevser, the Tesnim and the Salsebîl. The great Tûba tree grows in the highest Paradise; its branches fall into the seven other gardens.[2] This brief description will be sufficient

1. For further extracts from Sûfi writers see A Historical Enquiry concerning the Origin and Development of Sufiism, by R.A. Nicholson. The Journal of the Royal Asiatic Society, March, 1906.

2. See *History of Ottoman Poetry*, by E.G.W. Gibb, vol. i.

to show the nature of the Muslim heaven. That it was a glorified creation of the earth in eight degrees is evident. It was sensuous rather than metaphysical. The five worlds of the Sûfis are:

1. The "Plane of the Absolute Iavisible."
2. The "Relatively Invisible."
3. The "World of Similitudes."
4. The "Visible World" (or the plane of "Form, Generation and Corruption").
5. The "World of Man."

These Five Planes are often regarded as Three: the "Invisible," the "Intermediate," and the "Visible," or yet again as simply the "Visible" and "Invisible." Above the "Plane of the Absolute Invisible" is an infinity which we might, perhaps, compare with Dante's "Spaceless Empyrean." The Sûfis regarded the existence of the soul as pre-natal. Moreover that the full perception of Earthly Beauty was the remembrance of that Supreme Beauty in the Spiritual world. The body was the veil; but by ecstasy *(Hãl)* the soul could behold the Divine Mysteries. As Avicenna, in his poem on the soul, has written:

Lo, it was hurled
Midst the sign-posts and ruined abodes of this desolate world.
It weeps, when it thinks of its home and the peace it possessed,
With tears welling forth from its eyes without pausing or rest,
And with plaintive mourning it broodeth like one bereft Q'er such trace of its home as the fourfold winds have left.

Creation was regarded as the output of the All-Beautiful. The visible world and all therein was a reflection of the Divine, an ever-changing scene full of the Spirit of God. The following beautiful poem of Jãmi, from Yûsuf-wa-Zulaykhã, will illustrate the Sûfi's conception of the Beloved and His significance and relationship to His world of lovers:

> No mirror to reflect Its loveliness,
> Nor comb to touch Its locks; the morning breeze
> Ne'er stirred Its tresses; no collyrium
> Lent lustre to Its eyes; no rosy cheeks
> O'ershadowed by dark curls like hyacintsh.
> Nor peach-like down were there ...

To Itself it sang of love
In wordless measure. By Itself it cast
The die of love ...
One gleam fell from It on the Universe
And on the angels, and this single ray
Dazzled the angels, till their senses whirled
Like the revolving sky. In diverse forms
Each mirror showed it froth, and everywhere
Its praise was chanted in new harmonies.
The spirits who explore the depths
Of boundless seas, wherein the heavens swim
Like some small boat, cried with one mighty voice,
"Praise to the Lord of all the universe!"
His beauty everywhere doth show itself,
And through the forms of earthly beauties shines
Obscured as through a veil ...
Where'er thou seest a veil,
Beneath that veil He hides. Whatever heart
Doth yield to love, He charms it. In His love
The heart hath life. Longing for Him, the soul
Hath victory.[3]

3. Translation by Professor E.G. Browne.

Man was, therefore, a part of God, because he was a fragment of the Whole; or, better still, he was a divine emanation.[4] The Sûfi recognised this fact, and his supreme desire was to be reunited with the Beloved. His difficulty, however, was to bear in mind that his worship should ever be of God, and not of God's many beautiful forms. Love came in to his heart, and he endeavoured to recognise that earthly objects, however dear and beautiful they might be, were but lanterns where God's Light shone through. Here it must be readily admitted that Sûfiism often fails. The Sûfi poets were much given to excessive laudations of physical beauty, and we often find, with all the toleration and ingenuity we can bring to bear, that some of Hãfiz's lines are no more spiritual than Anacreon's, to whom he has been compared. We have a number of Sûfi words with a strictly Sûfi meaning; but it would not be wise to strain the analogy of earthly love

4. Compare the Alexandrian doctrine of Emanations. Also Jãmi's *Lawa'ih.* Translated by E.H. Whinfield and Mirzã Muhammad Kazvini.

too far and say that everything that Hãfiz wrote was spiritual. The Sûfi poets, for the most part, wrote about the Love of God in the terms applied to their beautiful women, for the simple reason that no one can write the celestial language and be understood at the same time. Is it to be wondered at that the Sûfis, still remembering their old love-songs, their old earthly delights in women dear to them, should find it difficult *not* to apply such names, such ideas even in their love of the One Beloved? Take those expressions literally and many of them are sensuous, but consider them as brave, strong strivings, fraught with much spiritual fervour, after God, and you at once annihilate prejudice and come very near understanding the meaning of Sûfiism. We need not fly to Mrs. Grundy and seek shelter under her hypocritical wing when some really devout and sincere Sûfi calls God 'the Eternal Darling" or sings about the Beloved's curls. In studying Sûfiism from Sûfi poetry we must always remember that Eastern poetry is essentially erotic in expression, but just as essentially symbolic in *meaning*. We must also bear in mind—and this point must have had its influence upon Sûfiism—that the Muslim's reward for having lived a good life, according to the teaching of Muhammad, was that he should enjoy an eternal *liaison* with lovely *houris*.

It may be questioned that if the earthly object of Love was a mere passing shadow of God, the man who loved that object was equally insignificant. And again, how can God be the All-One when, according to the Sûfi thesis, He divided Himself into creation? The part is not equal to the whole. These questions are easily answered. The stars shine in the sky, and on the bosom of the sea without diminution. Let the sea pass away, and the star-shadows pass away too; but the stars are still there. So when the world shall pass away it will only be the fading of innumerable shadows we call Humanity. God will still be there, and we shall still be there because we came alone from Him. There was a Voice that sounded in men and women, in mountains and in seas, in the beasts of the jungle and the swinging of the stars. It was the Voice of Love, the great reckoning in the Hereafter to which all things must go. That Voice to the Sûfi was God calling His lovers into one chamber, one mighty love-feast. Jãmi has expressed the finality of Love in the following lines:

> Gaze, till Gazing out of Gazing
> Grew to BEING Her I gaze on,
> She and I no more, but in One
> Undivided Being Blended.
> All that is not One must ever
> Suffer with the Wound of Absence;
> And whoever in Love's City
> Enter, finds but Room for one,
> And but in ONENESS Union.

The Rev. Professor W.R. Inge, in *Christian Mysticism,* has brought a good deal of adverse criticism to bear upon Sûfiism. He remarks: "The Sûfis or Mohammedan Mystics, use erotic language very freely, and appear, like true Asiatics, to have attempted to give a sacramental or symbolic character to the indulgence of their passions." The same writer accuses Emerson of "playing with pantheistic Mysticism of the Oriental type," and goes on to compare him with the Persian Sûfis on account of his self-deification. This critic, in his desire to defame the Sûfis, states that they are among the most shocking and blasphemous of the mystics, because they believe that state is present with them even in their earthly life. This, however, is no teaching of the Sûfis, and, rightly considered, we cannot even except the sayings of Bãyazid already referred to, because here he undoubtedly denies all claim to human personality, admitting God only. *Self*-deification is no teaching of the Sûfis. As the Buddhist's belief in Nirvan was a state only to be reached by degrees, after much striving and severe discipline, so was the fusion of the Beloved and His lover a belief and a beautiful hope far out on the spiritual horizon. Hadj Khan, in his interesting book *With the Pilgrims to Makkah,* briefly touches upon this sect and mentions "seven stages" in the spiritual growth of the Sûfi, and not an arrogant proclamation of Deity and man being coequal in the earthly existence. The gradually ascending scale of the Sûfi's heaven is another point in favour of this argument. "For the love that thou would'st find demands the sacrifice of self to the end that the heart may be filled with the passion to stand within the Holy of Holies, in which alone the mysteries of the True Beloved can be revealed unto thee." The average Sûfi was a poet. All that was beautiful was God to him. He tried to be nearer the Beautiful every day, and thus his soul swept on from flower to flower, higher and higher, until he was absorbed into the Divine.

We have now seen that Sûfiism is essentially a religion of Love without a creed or dogma. No merciless hells leap up in the Sûfi's beliefs. He has no *one way* theory for the life beyond: "The ways of God are as the number of the souls of men." There is splendid, magnificent broadmindedness in this Sûfi remark. This unsectarian teaching should be applied to every religion. It would tend to sweeten and deepen the thoughts of men, who would forget the petty nonessentials of creeds and dogmas, lost in the perception of the All-Beautiful.

IV. The Influence of Sufiism

This love here forms the centre which expandson all sides and into all regions.—**HEGEL**.

Although Jalãlu'ddin Rûmi' lived for fifty years in a Turkish city he scarcely ever used any Turkish words; but nevertheless his influence on Turkish poetry was very considerable. The Turkish poets of that day poured forth innumerable "spiritnal couplets" of a mystical nature. Indeed nearly all the 'uthoman poets were either Sûfis or men who wrote after the manner of the Persian Sûfis. Jalãl's son, Sultan Valad, wrote in Turkish the following concerning his father:

Wot ye well Mevlãna is of saints the Pole:
Whatsoever thing he sayeth, do in whole.
All his words are mercies from the Heavenly King:
Such that blind folks' eyes were opened, did they sing.

The Sûfi influence on Turkish poetry, many years after Jalãl's death, gradually weakened as time went on, and their poetry became less mystical. The French were probably responsible for this change to a certain extent.

Then, again, Sûfiism influenced the poetry of India; but in this case there was infuence on both sides, and the Sûfis probably borrowed some of the Buddhistic ideas, especially in regard to their later conception of Divine absorption. The following remark of Abû Bahu al-Shibli certainly points to the belief that the Sûfis inculcated certain ideas from the Vedanta Philosophy: "*Tasawwuf* is control of the faculties and *observance of the breaths*."

Sûfi poetry has greatly influenced Western thought. Many of the German mystics wrote as the Sûfi poets had written before them. Particularly might be mentioned Eckhart, Tauler and Suso. Concerning the last mentioned I may quote the following passage to demonstrate my meaning: "Earthly friends must needs endure to be distinct and separate from those whom they love; but Thou, O fathomless sweetness of all true love, meltest into the heart of Thy beloved, and pourest Thyself fully into the essence of his soul, that nothing of Thee remains outside, but Thou art joined and united most lovingly with Thy beloved." There was rapturous language both with the Persian and German mystics. The great difference between them was that the German mystics, for the most part, were ascetics, the Persians were not. Then again in the nineteenth century Hegel was loud in his praise of Jalãlu'ddin Rûmi, calling him a great thinker as well as a great poet, but somehow he seems to put Jalãl's Pantheism first, his Mysticism second. Surely this was putting the cart before the horse?

To trace the scope of the influence of Sûfi thought in England would be extremely interesting, but the limits of this little book will not admit of our doing so. The influence was at first among the few; but optimistic lovers of the East believe that Oriental thought is daily becoming of more interest to Western minds. The student knows that Edward

Fitz Gerald's rendering of Omar Khayyãm was anything but a faithful translation; that Fitz Gerald shook up Omar's words like so many dice and set them to the music of wine, roses, and pessimism. The Omar Khayyãm Club read Fitz Gerald, but not Omar Khayyãm, and in consequence they have fallen into the error of associating Omar with Bacchus. But, nevertheless, we must be grateful to Fitz Gerald. He has given us a great poem, and stirred, let us hope, many of his countless readers to a more faithful study of Persian poetry. The indefatigable Dr. Johnson has written the following on the Persian poet, who is the subject of our present volume: "He makes plain to the Pilgrim the secrets of the Way of Unity, and unveils the Mysteries of the Path of Eternal Truth." Concerning our modern poets I have quoted elsewhere a few lines of Mr. Arthur Symons on a dancing *dervish.* Many of the late Thomas Lake Harris's poems are of a Sûfi nature. In Mr. Stephen Phillip's beautiful poem "Marpessa," the following lines are full of Sûfi mysticism:

For they,

Seeking that perfect face beyond the world,

Approach in vision earthly semblances,

And touch, and at the shadows flee away.

It is interesting to note that at least one celebrated Englishman adopted the Sûfi teaching, I refer to Sir Richard Burton.[1] The Sûfis believed heart and soul in the beautiful lines of Cameons, the poet for whom Burton had so great an affection:

Do what thy manhood bids thee do, from none but self expect applause.

He noblest lives and noblest dies who makes and keeps his self made laws.

All other life is living death, a world where none but phantoms dwell;

A breath, a wind, a sound, a voice, a tinkling of the camel-bell.

V. Analysis of the Religion of Love

Put away the tale of love that travellers tell;

Do thou serve God with all thy might.

JALALU'DDIN RUMI

1. *Life of Sir Richard Burton.* 2 vols. by Thomas wright.

SUFIISM, then, is the religion of Love. Lafcadio Hearn tells us, in his inimitable way, that earthly love is brought about by the memories of innumerable loves in the past, a host of the phantoms of you seeking in your momentary ego the joy of Love over again. Schopenhauer, with much pride, quotes Rochefoucauld as having said that "love may be compared to a ghost since it is something we talk about but have never seen." Precisely; but this is no antagonistic statement, as Schopenhauer supposed. Rather than belitting the beauty of Love, it is an unconscious defence of a very great truth. Love can only be compared with Love. There is nothing else to compare it with. No one has seen Love, because no one has seen God. A little child plays at funerals and tenderly buries a dead butterfly, not because it understands the mystery of Death, but because Love prompted the action. And so we love without knowing the why and the wherefore. Scientists have already proved that first love is not controlled by either of the individuals loving; that it is but the expression of thousands of tendencies in past lives. That Love can be ever personal, ever 'limited to the individual, is unthinkable. We must recognise some day that those countless tendencies, those strivings after men and women seeming to hold our souls' affinities, were but the momentary finding of God in His creatures. We do not love a woman merely because she is pretty, possesses a pleasing mannerism. We love her because, in an indescribable way, she sings a song we alone can fully understand, a voice that lifts up our soul and makes it strong. We follow that Invisible Figure from land to land, from heart to heart, from Death into Life, on and on. When Love loves Love for its own sake, when the self is dead, we shall meet Him. We shall find the Beloved to be the Perfection, the realisation of that strong desire that made us lose ourselves in others. The more we lose ourselves in God the more we find Him. Men and women love and die. But Love is a Divine Essence working through and through innumerable lives for its own eternal glory. Personality is limited only to the finite world—

perhaps a phase of two beyond the grave. Even that is the sum-total of countless so-called personalities in the past. We love instinctively. If it was wholly physical then it dies with the death of the object. If it was infinitely more than that, if it was the love of Goodness and Purity and the Beautiful it lives on for ever. But these things live not eternally in humanity. They are parts of that all-pervading Essence—the Love Divine. Love God's light in men and women, and not the lanterns through which It shines, for human bodies must turn to dust; human memories, human desires, fade away. But the love of the All-Good, All-Beautiful remains, and when such is found in earthly love it is God finding Himself in you, and you in Him. That is the supreme teaching of Sûfiism, the religion of Love.

THE LIFE AND WORK OF JALALU'DDIN RÛMÎ

I. Life

JALALU'DDIN RÛMÎ was born at Balkh on September 30, 1207, A.D., or according to Mohammedan reckoning, in 604 A.H. His father, Bahau-'ddin, was a man of much learning, but gave offence to the reigning king by an attack on that monarch's innovations. Another account disputes this in the place of jealousy on the part of the king. Whatever the cause however, Bahau-'ddin left Balkh, together with his family, and settled at Nishapur. It was here that the celebrated Sûfi Faridu-ddin 'Attãr, presented young Jalãlu'ddin Rûmi with his Asramama[1], and informed his father that the child would some day become famous throughout the world. After the destruction of

1. *Book of Mysteries.*

Balkh the family went to Qonia,[2] an old Roman province, where the poet acquired his name Rûmi, or "the Roman." Young Jalãl must have been a child prodigy if we are to believe the many wonderful stories of his early days. At six years of age he is said to have seen visions, taught his playmates philosophy, and performed many marvellous feats, such as flying into the celestial regions. On the death of his father Jalãl took the professorial chair. He also founded an order of *Dervishes* known as *Maulavis*, where he authorised music and religious dance. When asked why he introduced singing and dance at a funeral, such practice being contrary to custom, Jalãl replied: "When the human spirit, after years of imprisonment in the cage and dungeon of the body, is at length set free, and wings its flight to the Source whence it came, is not this an occasion for rejoicings, thanks, and dancing?" Jalãl was an indomitable optimist. In his sayings, and still more in his poetry, we find an almost untrammelled ecstasy. The religious dances, known as Riza Kuli, may in some way account for Jalãl's occasional lack of care displayed in his poetry, and also for the outbursts not far removed from insanity. We are informed by Daulat Shãh that "there was a pillar in the Maulavi's house, and when he was drowned in the ocean of Love he used to take hold of that pillar and set himself turning round it." It was while turning round the pillar that he not infrequently dictated much of his poetry. As Mr. Arthur Symons has sung:

I turn until my sense,
Dizzied with waves of air,
Spins to a point intense,
And spires and centres there.[3]

We can well imagine Jalãl writing the following under the conditions just mentioned:

Come! Come! Thou art the Soul, the Soul so dear, revolving!
Come! Come! Thou art the Cedar, the Cedar's Spear, revolving!

3. *The Fool of the World.*

Oh, come! The well of Light up-bubbling springs;
And Morning Stars exult, in Gladness sheer, revolving !"[4]

In 1226 A.D. Jalãl was married at Lerenda to Gevher (Pearl). She bore two sons and died early in life. Jalãl married again and his second wife survived him.

II. Shams Tabraiz

A word must now be said about Shams Tabraiz, an intimate friend of Jalãl. We have sufficient evidence to prove that Jalãl's *nom de guerre,* was an actual person, and not a mythical creation on the part of the poet. This mysterious being, who fitted across Jalãl's life so tragically, seems to have had great personal influence over the poet, who went with him into solitary places and there discussed profound mysteries. The scholars of Jalãl looked upon the whole affair as an unworthy infatuation on the part of their Master, and on the part of Shams a shameful seduction. Their protests brought about

4. *The Festival of Spring.* Translated by the Rev. Prof. William Hastie.

the flight of Shams, who fled to Tabriz. But it was only a momentary separation. Jalãl followed this strange figure and brought him back again. Most of his lighter poetry was composed during this separation. Another disturbance, however, caused the departure of Shams to Damascus. we then have no clear record of him. Various legends, exist in regard to the death of this mysterious person. It may be safely stated, however that Shams met with a violent death, the exact nature of which it is impossible to say definitely.

This strange union is by no means unique in the history of the world's literature. The union however, in this particular case, is extremely diffcult to rightly fathom. We may reasonably infer that Jalãl's intense poetic temperament became fascinated by the dogmatic and powerful Shams. The very treatment of this friendship, both in the Lyrical Poems, and in the *Masnavi*, is Sûfi. The two following quotations, from many that might be cited, will prove sufficient to illustrate this point:

The face of Shamsuddin, Tabraiz s glory, is the sun
In whose track the cloud-like hearts are moving.
O Shams Tabraiz, beauty and glory of the horizons,
What king but is a beggar of thee with heart and soul?

III. The Stories of Al-Aflãki and the Death of Jalalu'd-din Rûmî[1]

The historian al-Aflãki, in his collection of anecdotes called Menaqibu 'l 'Arifin, [2] gives a number of stories relating to the miracles and wise sayings of Jalãl. Many of these miraculous performances were followed by the conversion of those who witnessed them. A marvel or a wise saying of Jalãl was generally accompanied by music and dance, which reminds us of the jubilations of the Indian gods after Rama's victories over his enemies. These stories, interesting enough in themselves, can scarcely be credited to such a learned man as Jalãl undoubtedly was. According to tradition he spoke to frogs and fishes, raised the

1. See the *Masnavi*, translated by Sir James W. Redhouse.
2. "The Acts of the Adepts."

dead to life, and at the same time very ignominiously lost his temper when a disciple who said, after having received Jalãl's instructions: "God willing." After all, the significance of Jalãl lies not in these rather lamentable fairy tales, but in the fruit of his work. Jalãl, like the Lord Buddha, suffered considerably from the addition of fabulous tales and fancies of no real moment to his teachings.

Al-Aflaki tells a pretty story concerning the tenderness of Jalãl for little children. As the poet passed by some children, they left their play and ran to him and bowed. Jalãl bowed in response. One little boy, some distance off, seeing the honour bestowed upon his playmates, cried to Jalãl: "Wait for me until I come!" And Jalãl waited and bowed to the little child. This story is worth far more than juggler's tricks.

Jalãlu'ddin Rûmî died at Qonia in 1273 A.D., praising God and leaving to the world a vast store of spiritual knowledge and many wise instructions to his son, Bahau'ddin Valad. It is very gratifying to note that at the death of Jalãl his mourners were of all creeds. A Christian was asked why he wept over a Muslim grave, and he replied: "We esteem him as the Moses, the David, the Jesus of our time; and we are his disciples, his adherents." This was indeed a splendid and worthy tribute to the memory of so great a man.

I hope I have already demonstrated that the very nature of Sûfi poetry is entirely lacking in creed or dogma, and certainly the great singer of the *Masnavi* has left in his songs a wealth of the wonder of Divine Love.

IV. The Nature and Significance of Jalalu'ddin Rûmî's Poetry

The Lyrical—We have already noted the acceptance of the *Asrarnama*. Among the other literary influences, according to Mr. Nicholson, we may note the poems of Sana'i, Sa'di, and Nizami. The fact that Jalãl's poetry sometimes faintly resembles Omar Khayyãm's is too slight to be of any value. Mr. Nicholson very ably sums up the nature of the *Masnavi* and *Divan* respectively: "The one is a majestic river, calm and deep, meandering through many a rich and varied landscape to the immeasurable ocean; the other a foaming torrent that leaps and plunges in the ethereal solitude of the hills." The poetry of Jalãl is not of equal merit. His work seldom if ever has the technical polish of Jãmî. There is too much of it; too much produced in the belief that all his poetry was inspired. He is fond of harping on certain words, and as far as the translations are concerned he has little sense of humour.[1] There was certainly room for a touch of humour in the poet's description of Iblis receiving from God a gift of beautiful women whereby to tempt mankind; but Jalãl entirely ignores it. These weaknesses are almost lost in the strength and purity and lyrical grandeur of many of Jalãl's poems. He carries us along on a torrent of heavenly music. The rhythmic swing of his wonderful dance is soul-stirring. We seem to move

1. Prof. C.E. Wilson informs me that Jalâl certainly had a very fair sense of humour, and that in the original there is often a clever and witty play on words.

exultantly, ecstatically to the sound of the poet's singing, far behind the silver stars into the Presence of the Beloved. With what reverence, with what a glow of smile and subtle suggestion he describes the Beauty of the Beloved! With what exquisite passion he foretells the Eternal Union! Then there is a lull in this fierce spiritual song, and Jalāl sings, ever so gently and with an infinite tenderness, about human tears being turned into "rainclouds." He sings about the meeting of two friends in Paradise, with the oft-repeated refrain, "Thou and I." There seems in this poem an indescribable and almost pathetic play on the idea of human friendship and the Divine Friendship, a yearning tenderness for that human shadow, passing shadow though it be. Jalāl appears to have the power of producing almost orchestral effects in his music of the Spheres. There is that terrific touch of Wagner about his poetry, and in those suggestive Wagner-pauses there is a tenderness of expression more touching, more truly great than the loud triumphant notes. Jalāl has truly said: "Our journey is to the Rose-

Garden of Union." He sang about the Divine Rose-Garden; but he did not forget to sing about the roses that fade and the human hearts that ache. We seem to see Jalãl ever bowing to the little child in all his wonderful singing.

The Masnavi—Jalãl is said to have been forty-three years engaged in writing the *Masnavi*. Often whole nights were spent in its composition, Jalãl reciting and his friend Hasan copying it down and sometimes singing portions of the verse in his beautiful voice. At the completion of the first book Hasan's wife died, and two years elapsed before the work was continued. The *Masnavi* is full of profound mysteries, and a most important book in the study of Sûfiism—mysteries which must, for the most part, be left to the discernment of the reader. Jalãl himself has said that great Love is silent. It is in Silence that we shall come to understand the supreme Mystery of Love that has no comparison. The key-note to the *Masnavi* may be found in the prologue to the first book. The poet here sings of the soul's longing to be united with the Beloved. The fact that he, and all other Sûfi poets, use as an analogy the love between man and woman renders the spiritual meaning extremely vague. We have, however, already considered this point in the introduction and it needs no further explanation. The *Masnavi* has all the pantheistic beauty of the Psalms, the music of the hills, the colour and scent of roses, the swaying of forests; but it has considerably more than that. These things of scent and form and colour are the Mirror of the Beloved; these earthy loves the journey down the valley into the Rose-Garden where the roses never fade and where Love is.

SELECTIONS FROM THE "DIVANE SHAMS TABRAIZ"

"I am Silent"

I am silent. Speak Thou, O Soul of Soul of Soul,
From desire of whose Face every atom grew articulate.

A Cry to the Beloved

Yestereve I delivered to a star tidings for thee: "Present," I said, "my service to that moon like form."

I bowed, I said: "Bear that service to the sun Who maketh hard rocks gold by his burning."

I bared my breast, I showed it the wounds: "Give news of me," I said, "to the Beloved whose drink is blood."

I rocked to and fro that the child, my heart, might become still;

A child sleeps when one sways the cradle.

Give my heart-babe milk, relieve us from its weeping,

O Thou, that helpest every moment a hundred helpless like me.

The heart's home, first to last, is Thy City of Union:

How long wilt Thou keep in exile this heart forlorn?

Remember God and Forget Self

O spirit, make thy head in search and seeking like the water of a stream,

And O reason, to gain Eternal Life tread everlastingly the way of Death.

Keep God in remembrance till self is forgotten,
That thou may be lost in the Called, without distraction of caller and call.

"The Prince of the Fair"

A garden—may its rose be in flower to Resurrection !

An idol—may the two worlds be scattered o'er his beauty!

The Prince of the Fair goes proudly forth to the chase at morning;

May our hearts fall a prey to the arrow of His glance!

From His eye what messages are passing continually to mine!

May my eyes be gladdened and filled with intoxication by His Message!

"My Body is Like the Moon"

My body is like the moon which is melting for Love,

My heart like Zuhra's[1] lute—may its strings be broken!

Look not on the moon's waning nor on Zuhra's broken state:

Behold the sweetness of his affection—may it wax a thousandfold!

1. The celestial Venus, and leader of the starry choirs to music. ·See R.A. Nicholson's note in *Selected Poems from the Divani Shamsi Tabriz*.

Mortality and Immortality

What a Bride is in the soul! By the reflection of Her face,

May the world be freshened and coloured like the hands of the newly married! [2]

Look not on the fleshy cheek which corrupts and decays,

Look on the spiritual cheek—may it be sweet and agreeable!

The dark body resembles a raven, and the body's world winter;

O in spite of these two unpleasants may there be Eternal Spring!

The Beloved the Divine Consoler

O Thou who art my soul's comfort in the season of sorrow,

O Thou who art my spirit's treasure in the bitterness of dearth!

That which the imagination has not conceived, that which the understanding has not seen,

2. A design traced in henna.

Visited my soul from Thee; hence in worship I turn toward Thee.

By Thy grace I keep fixed on Eternity my amorous gaze,

Except, O King, the pomps that perish lead me astray.

The favour of that one, who brings glad tidings of Thee,

Even without Thy summons, is sweeter in mine ear than songs.

If a never-ceasing bounty should offer kingdoms,

If a hidden treasure should set before me all that is,

I would bend down my soul, I would lay my face in the dust,

I would say, "Of all these the love of such an One for me!"

"Thou Art the Soul of the World"

Eternal Life, me thinks, is the time of Union,
Because Time, for me, hath no place There.

Life is the vessels, Union the clear draught in them;

Without Thee what does the pain of the vessels avail me?

I had twenty thousand desires ere this;

In passion for Him not even (care of) my safety remained.

By the help of His grace I am become safe, because

The unseen King saith to me, "Thou art the soul of the world."

"The Voice of Love"

Every moment the voice of Love is coming from left and right.

We are bound for heaven: who has a mind to sight-seeing?

We have been in heaven, we have been friends of the angels;

Thither, Sire, let us return, for that is our country.[3]

The Sea of Love

Mankind, like waterfowl, are sprung from the sea—the Sea of Soul;

Risen from that Sea, why should the bird make here his home?

Nay, we are pearls in that Sea, therein we all abide;

Else, why does wave follow wave from the Sea of Soul?

'Tis the time of Union's attainment, 'tis the time of Eternity's beauty,

'Tis the time of favour and largesse, 'tis the Ocean of perfect purity.

The billow of largesse hath appeared, the thunder of the Sea hath arrived,

The morn of blessedness hath dawned. Morn? No, 'tis the Light of God.

The Beauty of the Beloved

O Beloved, spiritual beauty is very fair and glorious,

But Thine own beauty and loveliness is another thing.

O Thou who art years describing Spirit,

Show one quality that is equal to His Essence.

Light waxes in the eye at the imagination of Him,

But in presence of His Union it is dimmed.

I stand open-mouthed in veneration of that beauty:

"God is most great" is on my heart's lips every moment.

The heart hath gotten an eye, constant in desire: of Thee.

O how that desire feeds heart and eye!

'Tis slave-caressing Thy Love has practised;

Else, where is the heart worthy of that love?

Every heart that has slept one night in Thy air Is like radiant day.

The Water of Eternal Life

Every form you see has its archetype in the placeless world;

If the form perished, no matter, since its Original is everlasting.

Every fair shape you have seen, every deep saying you have heard.

Be not cast down that it perished; for that is not so.

Whereas the Spring-head is undying, its branch gives water continually;

Since neither can cease, why are you lamenting? Conceive the Soul as a fountain, and these created things as rivers:

While the Fountain flows, the rivers run from it. Put grief out of your head and keep quaffing this River-water;

Do not think of the Water failing, for this water is without end.

Earthly Love and the Love Divine

'Twere better that the spirit which wears not true Love as a garment

Had not been: its being is but shame.

Without the dealing of Love there is no entrance to the Beloved.

'Tis Love and the Lover that live to all Eternity,

Set not thy heart on aught else: 'tis only borrowed,

How long wilt thou embrace a dead beloved ? Embrace the Soul which is embraced by nothing:

What was born of spring dies in autumn,
Love's rose-plot hath no aiding from the early spring.

"The House of Love"

This is the Lord of Heaven, who resembles Venus and the moon,
This is the House of Love, which has no bound or end.
Like a mirror, the soul has received Thy image in its heart;
The tip of Thy curl has sunk into my heart like a comb.
Forasmuch as the women cut their hands in Joseph's presence.
Come to me, O soul, for the Beloved is in the midst.

Love's Desire

Show Thy face, for I desire the orchard and the rose-garden:
Ope Thy lips, for I desire sugar in plenty.

O sun, show forth Thy face from the veil of cloud,
For I desire that radiant glowing countenance.

The Finding of the Beloved

I was on that day when the Names were not,
Nor any sign of existence endowed with name,
By me Names and Named were brought to view
On the day when there was not "I" and "We,"
For a sign, the tip of the Beloved's curl became a centre of revelation;
As yet the tip of that curl was not.
Cross and Christians, from end to end,
I surveyed; He was not on the Cross.
I went to the idol-temple, to the ancient pagoda;
No trace was visible there.
I went to the mountains of Herat and Khandahar;
I looked; He was not in that hill-and-dale.
I gazed into my own heart;
There I saw Him; He was nowhere else.

God Only

"None but God has contemplated the beauty of God."

This eye and that lamp are two lights, each individual,

When they came together, no one distinguished them.

The Moon-Soul and the Sea

At morning-tide a moon appeared in the sky,

And descended from the sky and gazed on me.

Like a falcon which snatches a bird at the time of hunting,

That moon snatched me up and coursed over the sky.

When I looked at myself, I saw myself no more,
Because in that moon my body became by grace even as soul.

When I travelled in soul, I saw naught save the moon,

Till the secret of the Eternal Theophany was revealed.

The nine spheres of heaven were all merged in that moon,

The vessel of my being was completely hidden in the sea.

The sea broke into waves, and again Wisdom rose

And cast abroad a voice; so it happened and thus it befell.

Foamed the sea, and at every foam-fleck

Something took figure and something was bodied forth.

Every foam-fleck of body, which received a sign from that sea,

Melted straightway and turned to spirit in this Ocean.

Life in Death

When my bier moveth on the day of Death,

Think not my heart is in this world.

Do not weep in devil's snare: that is woe.

When thou seest my hearse, cry not "Parted, parted!"

Union and meeting are mine in that hour.

If thou commit me to the grave, say not "Farewell, farewell!"

For the grave is a curtain hiding the communion of Paradise,

After beholding descent, consider resurrection;

Why should setting be injurious to the sun and moon?

To thee it seems a setting, but 'tis a rising;

Tho' the vault seems a prison, 'tis the release of the soul.

Shut thy mouth on this side and open it beyond,

For in placeless air will be thy triumphal song.

The Whole and the Part

Beware! do not keep, in a circle of reprobates,

Thine eye shut like a bud, thy mouth open like the rose.

The world resembles a mirror: thy Love is the perfect image:

O people, who has ever seen a part greater than the whole?

The Divine Friend

Look on me, for thou art my companion in the grave

On the night when thou shalt pass from shop and dwelling.

Thou shalt hear my hail in the hollow of the tomb: it shall become known to thee

That thou wast never concealed from mine eye.

I am as reason and intellect within thy bosom

At the time of joy and gladness, at the time of sorrow and distress.

In the hour when the intellectual lamp is lighted,

What a pean goes up from the dead men in the tombs!

Aspiration

Haste, haste! for we too, O soul, are coming

From this world of severance to that world of Union.

O how long shall we, like children, in the earthly sphere
Fill our lap with dust and stones and sherds?
Let us give up the earth and fly heavenwards,
Let us flee from childhood to the banquet of men.
Behold how the earthly frame has entrapped thee!
Rend the sack and raise thy head clear.

"I will Cherish the Soul"

"I am a painter, a maker of pictures; every moment I shape a beauteous form,
And then in Thy presence I melt them all away.
I call up a hundred phantoms and indue them with a spirit;
When I behold Thy phantom, I cast them in the fire."
Lo! I will cherish the soul, because it has a perfume of Thee.
Every drop of blood which proceeds from me is saying to Thy dust:
"I am one colour with Thy love, I am a partner of Thy affection."

In the house of water and clay this heart is desolate without Thee;

O Beloved, enter the house, or I will leave it.

"This is Love"

This is Love: to fly heavenward,
To rend, every instant, a hundred veils.
The first moment, to renounce Life:
The last step, to feel without feet.
To regard this world as invisible,
Not to see what appears to one's self.
"O heart," I said, "may it bless thee
To have entered the circle of lovers,
To look beyond the range of the eye,
To penetrate the windings of the bosom!
Whence did this breath come to thee, O my soul,
Whence this throbbing, O my heart?"

The Journey to the Beloved

O lovers, O lovers, it is time to abandon the world:

The drum of departure reaches my spiritual ear from heaven.

Behold, the driver has risen and made ready his files of camels,

And begged us to acquit him of blame : why, O travellers, are you asleep?

These sounds before and behind are the din of departure and of the camel-bells;

With each moment a soul and spirit is setting off into the Void.

From these inverted candles, from these blue awnings.

There has come forth a wondrous people, that the mysteries may be revealed.

A heavy slumber fell upon thee from the circling spheres:

Alas, for this life so light, beware of this slumber so heavy!

O soul, seek the Beloved, O friend, seek the Friend,

O watchman, be wakeful: it behoves not a watchman to sleep.

The Day of Resurrection

On every side is clamour and tumult, in every street are candles and torches,

For to-night the teeming world gives birth to the World Everlasting.

Thou wert dust and art spirit, thou wert ignorant and art wise.

He who has led thee thus far will lead thee further also.

How pleasant are the paints He makes thee suffer while He gently draws thee to Himself!

The Return of the Beloved

Always at night returns the Beloved: do not eat opium to-night;

Close your mouth against food, that you may taste the sweetness of the mouth.

Lo, the cup bearer is no tyrant, and in his assembly there is a circle:

Come into the circle, be seated; how long will you regard the revolution (of Time)?

Why, when God's earth is so wide, have you fallen asleep in a prison?

Avoid entangled thoughts, that you may see the explanation of Paradise.

Refrain from speaking, that you may win speech hereafter.

Abandon life and the world, that you may behold the Life of the world.

The Call of the Beloved

Every morning a voice comes to thee from heaven:

"When thou lay'st the dust of the way, thou win'st thy way to the goal."

On the road to the *Ka'bah* of Union, lo, in every thorn-bush

Are thousands slain of desire who manfully yielded up their lives.

Thousands sank wounded on this path, to whom there came not

A breath of the fragrance of Union, a token from the neighbourhood of the Friend.

"The Banquet of Union"

In memory of the banquet of Union, in yearning for His beauty

They are fallen bewildered by the wine Thou knowest.

How sweet, in the hope of Him, on the threshold of His Abode,

For the sake of seeing His face, to bring night round to day!

Illumine thy bodily senses by the Light of the soul:

Look not in the world for bliss and fortune, since thou wilt not find them;

Seek bliss in both worlds by serving Him,

Put away the tale of Love that travellers tell;

Do thou serve God with all thy might.

"Be Silent"

Be silent that the Lord who gave thee language may speak,

For as He fashioned a door and lock, He has also made a key.

"Thou Didst go to the Rose-Garden"

At last thou hast departed and gone to the Unseen;

Tis marvellous by what way thou wentest from the world.

Thou didst strongly shake thy wings and feathers, and having broken thy cage

Didst take to the air and journey towards the world of Soul.

Thou wert a favourite falcon, kept in captivity by an old woman:

When thou heard'st the falcon-drum thou didst fly away into the Void.

Thou wert a love-lorn nightingale among owls:

The scent of the Rose-Garden reached thee, and thou didst go to the Rose-Garden.

"The World Gave Thee False Clues"

The world gave thee false clues, like a ghoul:

Thou took'st no heed of the clue, but wentest to that which is without a clue.

Since thou art now the sun, why dost thou wear a tiara?

Why seek a girdle, since thou art gone from the middle?

I have heard that thou art gazing with distorted eyes upon thy soul:

Why dost thou gaze on thy soul, since thou art gone to the Soul of soul?

O heart, what a wondrous bird art thou, that in chase of divine rewards

Thou didst fly with two wings to the spear-point, like a shield!

The rose flees from autumn—O what a fearless rose art thou,

Who didst go loitering along in the presence of the autumn wind!

Falling like rain from heaven upon the roof of the terrestrial world

Thou didst run in every direction till thou didst escape by conduit.

Be silent and free from the pain of speech: do not slumber,

Since thou hast taken refuge with so loving a Friend.

"He Comes"

He comes, a moon whose like the sky ne'er saw, awake or dreaming,

Crowned with Eternal Flame no flood can lay.

Lo, from the flagon of Thy Love, O Lord, my soul is swimming,

And ruined all my body's house of clay!

When first the Giver of the grape my lonely heart befriended,

Wine fired my bosom and my veins filled up,

But when His image all mine eye possessed, a voice descended:

"Well done, O sovereign Wine and peerless Cup!

Love's mighty arm from roof to base each dark abode is hewing

Where chinks reluctant catch a golden ray.

My heart, when Love's sea of a sudden burst into its viewing,

Leaped headlong in, with "Find me now who may!"

"The Road be Thine Towards the Shrine"

O honoured guest in Love's high feast, O bird of the angel-sphere,

'Tis cause to weep, if thou wilt keep thy habitation here.

A voice at morn to thee is borne—God whispers to the soul—

"If on the way the dust thou lay, thou soon wilt gain the goal."

The road be thine toward the Shrine! and lo, in bush and briar,

The many slain of Love and pain in flower of young desire,

Who on the track fell wounded back and saw not, ere the end,

A ray of bliss, a touch, a kiss, a token of the Friend!

Thy Rose

Our Sweetnesses all blent in Thee,

Give infant lips their smiles benign.

Thou crushest me to drops of Rose

Nor 'neath the press do I repine.

In Thy sweet Pain is pain forgot;

For I, Thy Rose, had this design.

Thou bad'st me blossom on Thy Robe,
And mad'st me for all eyes Thy sign.
And when Thou pour'st me on the world,
It blows in beauty, all Divine.

"I Saw the Winter Weaving"

I saw the winter weaving from flakes a robe of Death;
And the spring found earth in mourning, all naked, lone, and bare.
I heard Time's loom a-whirring that wove the Sun's dim Veil;
I saw a worm a-weaving in Life-threads its own lair.
I saw the Great was the Smallest, and saw the Smallest Great;
For God had set His likeness on all the things that were.

"Love Sounds the Music of the Spheres"

O, soul, if thou, too, wouldst be free,
Then love the Love that shuts thee in.

'Tis Love that twisteth every snare;
'Tis Love that snaps the bond of sin;
Love sounds the Music of the Spheres;
Love echoes through Earth's harshest din.

* * * *

The world is God's pure mirror clear,
To eyes when free from clouds within.
With Love's own eyes the Mirror view,
And there see God to self akin.

"The Souls Love-Moved"

The souls love-moved are circling on,
Like streams to their great Ocean King.
Thou art the Sun of all men's thoughts;
Thy kisses are the flowers of spring.
The dawn is pale from yearning Love;
The moon in tears is sorrowing.
Thou art the Rose, and deep for Thee,
In sighs, the nightingales still sing.

The Beloved All in All

My Soul sends up to Heaven each night the cry of Love!

God's starry Beauty draws with might the cry of Love!

Bright sun and moon each morn dance in my Heart at Dawn:

And waking me at daylight, excite the cry of Love!

On every meadow glancing, I see God's sunbeams play;

And all Creation's wonders excite the cry of Love!

I, All in All becoming, now clear see God in All;

And up from Union yearning, takes flight the cry of Love!

"Thou and I"

Happy the moment when we are seated in the Palace, thou and I,

With two forms and with two figures but with one soul, thou and I.

The colours of the grove and the voice of the birds will bestow immortality

At the time when we come into the garden, thou and I.

The stars of heaven will come to gaze upon us;

We shall show them the moon itself, thou and I.

Thou and I, individuals no more, shall be mingled in ecstasy,

Joyful, and secure from foolish babble, thou and I.

All the bright-plumed birds of heaven will devour their hearts with envy

In the place where we shall laugh in such a fashion, thou and I.

This is the greatest wonder, that thou and I, sitting here in the same nook,

Are at this moment both in 'Iraq and Khorasan, thou and I.

SELECTIONS FROM THE "MASNAVI"

Sorrow Quenched in the Beloved

Through grief my days are as labour and sorrow,
My days move on, hand in hand with anguish.
Yet, though my days vanish thus, 'tis no matter,
Do Thou abide, O Incomparable Pure One.

The Music of Love

Hail to thee, then, O LOVE, sweet madness!
Thou who healest all our infirmities!
Who art the Physician of our pride and self-conceit!
Who art our Plato and our Galen!
Love exalts our earthly bodies to heaven,
And makes the very hills to dance with joy!
O lover, 'twas Love that gave life to Mount Sinai,

When "it quaked, and Moses fell down in a swoon."
Did my Beloved only touch me with His lips,
I too, like a flute, would burst out into melody.

"When the Rose has Faded"

When the rose has faded and the garden is withered,
The song of the nightingale is no longer to be heard.
The BELOVED is all in all, the lover only veils Him;
The BELOVED is all that lives, the lover a dead thing.
When the lover feels no longer LOVE'S quickening,
He becomes like a bird who has lost its wings, Alas!
How can I retain my senses about me,
When the BELOVED shows not the Light of His countenance?

The Silence of Love

Love is the astrolabe of God's mysteries.
A lover may hanker after this love or that love,

But at the last he is drawn to the KING of Love.
However much we describe and explain Love,
When we fall in love we are ashamed of our words.
Explanation by the tongue makes most things clear,
But Love unexplained is better.

Earthly Love Essential to the Love Divine

In one 'twas said, "Leave power and weakness alone;
Whatever withdraws thine eyes from God is an idol."
In one 'twas said, "Quench not thy earthy torch,
That it may be a light to lighten mankind.
If thou neglectest regard and care for it,
Thou wilt quench at midnight the lamp of Union."

The Eternal Splendour of the Beloved

Why dost Thou flee from the cries of us on earth?
Why pourest Thou sorrow on the heart of the sorrowful?

O Thou who, as each new dawns from the east,
Art seen uprising anew, like a bright fountain!
What excuse makest Thou for Thy witcheries?
O Thou whose lips are sweeter than sugar,
Thou that ever renewest the life of this old world,
Hear the cry of this lifeless body and heart!

Woman

Woman is a ray of God, not a mere mistress,
The Creator's Self, as it were, not a mere creature!

The Divine Union

Mustafa[1] became beside himself at that sweet call,
His prayer failed on "the night of the early morning halt."
He lifted not head from that blissful sleep,[2]
So that his morning prayer was put off till noon.

1. Muhammad Mustafa (Peace be up on him)

usrat Ali asri

2. The night of his marriage with Safiyya

On that, his wedding night, in the presence of his bride,

His pure soul attained to kiss her hands.

Love and mistress are both veiled and hidden.

Impute it not a fault if I call Him "Bride."

"He Knows About it all"[3]

He who is from head to foot a perfect rose or lily,

To him spring brings rejoicing.

The useless thorn desires the autumn,

That autumn may associate itself with the garden;

And hide the rose's beauty and the thorn's shame,

That men may not see the bloom of the one and the other's shame;

The common stone and pure ruby may appear all as one.

True, the Gardener knows the difference in the autumn,

But the sight of *One* is better than the world's sight.

3. See *Rubaiyat* of Omar Khayyām, translated by Edward Fitz-Gerald, second edition, quatrain lxx.

Resignation the way to Perfection

Whoso recognises and confesses his own defects
Is hastening in the way that leads to Perfection!
But he advances not towards the Almighty
Who fancies himself to be perfect.

Love the Source of Light Rather than Vanishing Form

Whatsoever is perceived by sense He annuls,
But He stablishes that which is hidden from the senses.
The lover's love is visible, his Beloved hidden.
The Friend is absent, the distraction He causes present.
Renounce these affections for outward forms,
Love depends not on outward form or face.
Whatever is beloved is not a mere empty form,
Whether your beloved be of the earth or heaven.
Whatever is the form you have fallen in love with—
Why do you forsake it the moment life leaves it?

The form[4] is still there; whence then this disgust as it?

Ah! lover, consider well what is really your beloved,

If a thing perceived by outward senses is the beloved,

Then all who retain their senses must still love it;

And since Love increases constancy,

How can constancy fail while form abides?

But the truth is, the sun's beams strike the wall,

And the wall only reflects that borrowed light.

Why give your heart to mere stones, O simpleton?

Go! Seek the Source of Light which shineth always!

The Religion of Love

The sect of lovers is distinct from all others,

Lovers have a religion and a faith of their own.

Though the ruby has no stamp, what matters it?

Love is fearless in the midst of the sea of fear.

4. "Form" here is used rather as soul, the love behind the decaying body.

"Pain is a Treasure"

Pain is a treasure, for it contains mercies;

The kernel is soft when the rind is scraped off.

O brother, the place of darkness and cold

Is the fountain of Life and the cup of ecstasy.

So also is endurance of pain and sickness and disease.

For from abasement proceeds exaltation.

The spring seasons are hidden in the autumns,

And the autumns are charged with springs.

Spirit Greater than Form

If spiritual manifestations had been sufficient,

The creation of the world had been needless and vain.

If spiritual thought were equivalent to love of God,

Outward forms of temples and prayers would not exist.

The Beloved Compared to "A Sweet Garden"

"We bow down our heads before His edict and ordinance,
We stake precious life to gain His favour.
While the thought of the Beloved fills our hearts,
All our work is to do Him service and spend life for Him.
Wherever He kindles His destructive torch,
Myriads of lovers' souls are burnt therewith.
The lovers who dwell within the sanctuary
Are moths burnt with the torch of the Beloved's face."
O heart, haste thither, for God will shine upon you,
And seem to you a sweet garden instead of a terror.
He will infuse into your soul a new Soul,
So as to fill you, like a goblet, with wine.
Take up your abode in His Soul!
Take up your abode in heaven. O bright full moon!

Like the heavenly Scribe, He will open your heart's book
That He may reveal mysteries unto you.

"Behold the Water of Waters!"

The sea itself is one thing, the foam another;
Neglect the foam, and regard the sea with your eyes.
Waves of foam rise from the sea night and day.
You look at the foam ripples and not at the mighty sea.
We, like boats, are tossed hither and thither,
We are blind though we are on the bright ocean.
Ah! you who are asleep in the boat of the body,
You see the water; behold the Water of waters!
Under the water you see there is another Water moving it.
Within the spirit is a Spirit that calls it.

When you have accepted the Ligh, O beloved.

When you behold what is veiled without a veil,
Like a star you will walk upon the heavens.

Where Love is

A damsel said to her lover, "O fond youth,
You have visited many cities in your travels;
Which of those cities seems most delightful to you?"
He made answer, "The city wherein my love dwells,
In whatever nook my queen alights;
Though it be as the eye of a needle, 'tis a wide plain;
Wherever her Yusuf-like[5] face shines as a moon,
Though it be the bottom of a well, 'tis Paradise.
With thee, my love, hell itself were heaven.
With thee a prison would be a rose-garden.
With thee hell would be a mansion of delight,
Without thee lilies and roses would be as flames of fire!"

5. Joseph, a name frequently used by Persian poets, irrespective of gender, to symbolise the ideal type of human beauty.

The Love of the Beloved

No lover ever seeks union with his beloved,
But his beloved is also seeking union with him.
But the lover's love[6] makes his body lean,
While the Beloved's love makes her fair and lusty.
When in *this* heart the lightning spark of love arises,
Be sure this Love is reciprocated in *that* heart.
When the Love of God arises in thy heart,
Without doubt God also feels love for thee.

The Love of the Soul and the Love of the Body

The Love of the soul is for Life and the Living One,
Because its origin is the Soul not bound to place.
The Love of the soul is for wisdom and knowledge,
That of the body for houses, gardens, and vineyards;
The love of the soul is for things exalted on high,
That of the body for acquisition of goods and food.

6. Earthly love.

The Love, too, of Him on high is directed to the soul:

Know this, for "He loves them that love Him."[7]

The sum is this: that whoso seeks another,

The soul of that other who is sought inclines to him.

"O Love, Love, and Heart's Desire of Love!"

O Israfil of the resurrection day of Love!

O Love, Love, and heart's desire of Love!

Let thy first boon to me be this:

To lend thine ear to my orisons,

Though thou knowest my condition clearly,

O protector of slaves, listen to my speech.

A thousand times, O prince incomparable,

Has my reason taken flight in desire to see thee,

And to hear thee and to listen to thy words,

7. Qur'an-e-Majeed.

And to behold thy life-giving smiles.
Thy inclining thine ear to my supplications
Is as a caress to my misguided soul.

Destroy not Earthly Beauty: It Beautifies the Soul

Tear not thy plumage off, it cannot be replaced;
Disfigure not thy face in wantonness, O fair one!
That face which is bright as the forenoon sun—
To disfigure it were a grievous sin.
'Twere paganism to mar such a face as thine!
The moon itself would weep to lose sight of it!
Knowest thou not the beauty of thine own face?
Quit this temper that leads thee to war with thyself!
It is the claws of thine own foolish thoughts
That in spite wound the face of thy quiet soul.
Know such thoughts to be claws fraught with poison.
Which score deep wounds on the face of thy soul.

The Devil Makes use of the Beauty of Women

Thus spake cursed Iblis to the Almighty,
"I want a mighty trap to catch human game withal!"
God give him gold and silver and troops and horses,
Saying, "You can catch my creatures with these."
Iblis said, "Bravo!" but at the same time hung his lip,
And frowned sourly like a bitter orange.
Then God offered gold and jewels from precious mines
To that laggard in the faith,
Saying, "Take these other traps, O cursed one."
But Iblis said, "Give me more, O blessed Defender."
God gave him succulent and sweet and costly wines,
And also store of silken garments.
But Iblis said, "O Lord, I want more aids than these,
In order to bind men in my twisted rope
So firmly that Thy adorers, who are valiant men,

May not, man-like, break my bonds asunder."

When at last God showed him the beauty of women,

Which bereaves men of reason and self-control,

Then Iblis clapped his hands and began to dance,

Saying, "Give me these; I shall quickly prevail with these!"[8]

"Lovers and Beloved have Both Perished"

Lovers and beloved have both perished;

And not themselves only, but their love as well,

'Tis God alone who agitates these nonentities,

Making one nonentity fall in love with another.

In the heart that is no heart envy comes to a head,

Thus Being troubles nonentity.[9]

8. The meaning of this poem is strictly allegorical. We must not infer that the All-Good would be a party to the evil designs of the Devil. No material gifts, however seductive, could succeed in stamping out the Divine Presence in His creatures.

9. At first sight there seems to be Omarian pessimism in this poem. In reality it signifies that all love is One, which ahines through the ever-vanishing lanterns of the world.

"O Angels, Bring him Back to me"

"O angels, bring him back to me.
Since the eyes of his heart were set on Hope,
Without care for consequence I set him free,
And draw the pen through the record of his sins!"

Self-Aggrandisement and Vainglory no Part of Love

A lover was once admitted to the presence of his mistress, but, instead of embracing her, he pulled out a paper of sonnets and read them to her, describing her perfections and charms and his own love towards her at length. His mistress said to him, "You are now in my presence, and these lovers' sighs and invocations are a waste of time. It is not the part of a true lover to waste his time in this way. It shows that I am not the real object of your affection, but that what you really love is your own effusions and ecstatic raptures. I see, as it were, the water which I have longed for before me, and yet you withhold it. I am, as it were, in Bulgaria, and the object of your love is in Cathay. One who is really loved is the single object of her lover, the Alpha and Omega of his desires. As for you, you are wrapped up in your own amorous raptures, depending on the varying states of your own feelings, instead of being wrapped up in me."

"I am Thine, and Thou Art Mine!"

Eternal Life is gained by utter abandonment of one's own life. When God appears to His ardent lover the lover is absorbed in Him, and not so much as a hair of the lover remains. True lovers are as shadows, and when the sun shines in glory the shadows vanish away. He is a true lover to God to whom God says, "I am thine, and thou art Mine!"

Love Needs no Mediator

When one has attained Union with God he has no need of intermediaries. Prophets and Apostles are needed as links to connect ordinary man with God, but he who hears the "inner voice" within him has no need to listen to outward words. even of apostles. Although that intercession is himself dwelling in God, yet my state is higher and more lovely than his. Though he is God's agent, yet I desire not his intercession to save me from evil sent me by God, for evil at God's hand seems to me good. What seems mercy and kindness to the vulgar seems wrath and vengeance to God-intoxicated saints.

Humanity the Reflection of the Beloved

Parrots are taught to speak without understanding the words. The method is to palce a mirror between the parot and the trainer. The trainer, hidden by the mirror, utters the words, and the parrot, seeing his own reflection in the mirror, fancies another parrot is speaking, and imitates all that is said by the trainer behind the mirror. So God uses prophets and saints as mirrors whereby to instruct men, *viz.*, the bodies of these saints and prophets; and men, when they hear the words proceeding from these mirrors, are utterly ignorant that they are really being spoken by "Universal Reason" or the "Word of God" behind the mirror of the saints.

"Earthly Forms"

Earthly forms are only shadows of the Sun of Truth—a cradle for babes, but too small to hold those who have grown to spiritual manhood.

"The Beatific Vision of Eternal Truth"

The end and object of all negations is to attain to subsequent affirmation, as the negation in the creed, "There is no God," finds its complement and purpose in the affirmation "but God." Just so the purpose of negation of self is to clear the way for the apprehension of the fact that there is no existence but the One. The intoxication of Life and its pleasures and occupations veils the Truth from men's eyes, and they ought to pass on to the spiritual intoxication which makes men beside themselves and lifts them to the beatific vision of eternal Truth.

The Wine Everlasting

O babbler, while thy soul is drunk with mere date-wine,

Thy spirit hath not tasted the genuine grapes.
For the token of thy having seen that divine Light
Is this, to withdraw thyself from the house of pride.

Be Lost in the Beauty of the Beloved

When those Egyptian women sacrificed their reason,
They penetrated the mansion of Joseph's love;
The Cup-bearer of Life bore away their reason,
They were filled with wisdom of the world without end.
Joseph's beauty was only an offshoot of God's beauty:
Be lost, then, in God's beauty more than those women.

"What Ear has told You Falsely"

What ear has told you falsely eye will tell trully.
Then ear, too, will acquire the properties of an eye;
Your ears, now worthless as wool, will become gems;

Yea, your whole body will become a mirror,

It will be as an eye of a bright gem in your bosom.

First the hearing of the ear enables you to form ideas,

Then these ideas guide you to the Beloved.

Strive, then, to increase the number of these ideas,

That they may guide you, like Majnun, to the Beloved.

"There is a Place of Refuge"

Yea, O sleeping heart, know the kingdom that endures not

For ever and ever is only a mere dream.

I marvel how long you will indulge in vain illusion,

Which has seized you by the throat like a headsman.

Know that even in this world there is a place of refuge;

Hearken not to the unbeliever who denies it.

His argument is this: he says again and again,

"If there were aught beyond this life we should see it."

But if the child see not the state of reason,
Does the man of reason therefore forsake reason?
And if the man of reason sees not the state of Love,
Is the blessed moon of Love thereby eclipsed?

The Lover's Cry to the Beloved

"My back is broken by the conflict of my thoughts;
O Beloved One, come and stroke my head in mercy!
The palm of Thy hand on my head gives me rest,
Thy hand is a sign of Thy bounteous providence.
Remove not Thy shadow from my head,
I am afflicted, afflicted, afflicted!
Sleep has deserted my eyes
Through my longing for Thee, O Envy of cypresses!

O take my life, Thou art the Source of Life!
For apart from Thee I am wearied of my life;
I am a lover well versed in lovers' madness,
I am weary of learning and sense."

Sorrow Turned to Joy

"He who extracts the rose from the thorn
Can also turn this winter into spring.
He who exalts the heads of the cypresses
Is able also out of sadness to bring joy."

The Gifts of the Beloved

Where will you find one more liberal than God?
He buys the worthless rubbish which is your wealth,
He pays you the Light that illumines your heart.
He accepts these frozen and lifeless bodies of yours,
And gives you a kingdom beyond what you dream of,
He takes a few drops of your tears,
And gives you the Divine Fount sweeter than sugar.
He takes your sighs fraught with grief and sadness,
And for each sigh gives rank in heaven as interest.
In return for the sigh-wind that raised tear-clouds.

God gave Abraham the title of "Father of the Faithfuls."

"Thou Art Hidden from Us"

Thou art hidden from us, though the heavens are filled
With Thy Light, which is brighter than sun and moon!
Thou art hidden, yet revealest our hidden secrets!
Thou art the Source that causes our rivers to flow.
Thou art hidden in Thy essence, but seen by Thy bounties.
Thou art like the water, and we like the millstone.
Thou art like the wind, and we like the dust;
The wind is unseen, but the dust is seen by all.
Thou art the Spring, and we the sweet green garden;
Spring is not seen, though its gifts are seen.
Thou art as the Soul, we as hand and foot;
Soul instructs hand and foot to hold and take.
Thou art as Reason, we like the tongue;

'Tis reason that teaches the tongue to speak.
Thou art as Joy, and we are laughing;
The laughter is the consequence of the joy.
Our every motion every moment testifies,
For it proves the presence of the Everlasting God.

"Exert Yourselves"

'Trust in God, yet tie the camel's leg.'
Hear the adage, 'The worker is the friend of God;'
Through trust in Providence neglect not to use means.
Go, O Fatalists, practise trust with self-exertion,
Exert yourself to attain your objects, bit by bit.
In order to succeed, strive and exert yourselves;
If you strive not for your objects, ye are fools."

The Wisdom of the Weak

"O friends, God has given me inspiration.
Oftentimes strong counsel is suggested to the weak.

The wit taught by God to the bee
Is withheld from the lion and the wild ass.
It fills its cells with liquid sweets,
For God opens the door of this knowledge to it.
The skill taught by God to the silkworm
Is a learning beyond the reach of the elephant.
The earthly Adam was taught of God names,
So that his glory reached the seventh heaven.
He laid low the name and fame of the angels,
Yet blind indeed are they whom God dooms to doubt!"

White Nights

Every night Thou freest our spirits from the body
And its snare, making them pure as rased tablets.
Every night spirits are released from this cage,
And set free, neither lording it nor lorded over.
At night prisoners are unaware of their prison,
At night kings are unaware of their majesty.

"The Kingly Soul"

The kingly soul lays waste the body,
And after its destruction he builds it anew.
Happy the soul who for love of God
Has lavished family, wealth, and goods!—
Has destroyed its house to find the Hidden Treasure,
And with that Treasure has rebuilt it in fairer sort;
Has dammed up the stream and cleansed the channel,
And then turned a fresh stream into the channel.

Saint and Hypocrite

Watch the face of each one, regard it well,
It may be by serving thou wilt recognise Truth's face.
As there are many demons with men's faces,
It is wrong to join hand with every one.
When the fowler sounds his decoy whistle,
That the birds may be beguiled by that snare,

The birds hear that call simulating a bird's call,
And, descending from the air, find net and knife.
So vile hypocrites steal the language of *Dervishes,*
In order to beguile the simple with their trickery.
The works of the righteous are light and heat,
The works of the evil treachery and shamelessness.
They make stuffed lions to scare the simple,
They give the title of Muhammad to false Musailima.
But Musailima retained the name of "Liar,"
And Muhammad that of "Sublimest of beings."
That wine of God (the righteous) yields a perfume of musk;
Other wine (the evil) is reserved for penalties and pains.

Harshness and Adoration

Let me then, I say, make complaint
Of the severity of that Fickle Fair One.
I cry, and my cries sound sweet in His ear;

He requires from the two worlds cries and groans.
How shall I not wail under His chastening hand?
How shall I not be in the number of those bewitched by Him?
How shall I be other than night without His day?
Without the vision of His face that illumes the day?
His bitters are very sweets to my soul,
I am enamoured of my own grief and pain,
For it makes me well-pleasing to my peerless King.
I use the dust of my grief as salve for my eyes,
That my eyes, like seas, may team with pearls.

The Divine Absorption

Do me justice, O Thou who are the glory of the just,
Who art the throne, and I the lintel of Thy door!
But, in sober truth, where are throne and door-way?
Where are "We" and "I"? There where our Beloved is!
O Thou, who art exempt from "Us" and "Me",

Who pervadest the spirits of all men and women;
When man and woman become one, Thou art that One!
When their union is dissolved, lo! Thou abidest!
Thou hast made these "Us" and "Me" for this purpose,
To wit, to play chess with them by Thyself.
When Thou shalt become one entity with "Us" and "You",
Then wilt Thou show true affection for these lovers.
When these "We" and "Ye", shall all become One Soul,
Then they will be lost and absorbed in the "Beloved".

Love More than Sorrow and Joy

Come then, O Lord!
Who art exalted above description and explanation!
It it possible for the bodily eye to behold Thee?
Can mind of man conceive Thy frowns and Thy smiles?

Are hearts, when bewitched by Thy smiles and frowns,

In a fit state to see the vision of Thyself?

When our hearts are bewitched by Thy smiles and frowns,

Can we gain Life from these two alternating states?

The fertile garden of Love, as it is boundless,

Contains other fruits besides joy and sorrow.

The true lover is exalted above these two states,

He is fresh and green independently of autumn or spring!

Pay tithe on Thy beauty, O Beauteous One!

Tell forth the tale of the Beloved, every whit!

"The Heart of the Harper"

The heart of the harper was emancipated.

Like a soul he was freed from weeping and rejoicing,

His old life died, and he was regenerated.

Amazement fell upon him at that moment,

For he was exalted above earth and heaven,
An uplifting of the heart surpassing all uplifting,
I cannot describe it; if you can, say on!
Ecstasy and words beyond all ecstatic words;—
Immersion in the glory of the Lord of glory!
Immersion wherefrom was no extrication,—
As it were identification with the Very Ocean!

"When Night Returns"

When night returns and 'tis the time of the sky's levee,
The stars that were hidden come forth to their work.
The people of the world lie unconscious,
With veils drawn over their faces, and asleep, But
when the morn shall brut forth and the sun arise
Every creature will raise its head from its couch;
To the unconscious God will restore consciousness;
They will stand in rings as slaves with rings in ears;

Dancing and clapping hands with songs of praise,
Singing with joy, "Our Lord hath restored us to life!"

Separation

Nothing is bitterer than severance from Thee,
Without Thy shelter there is naught but perplexity.
Our worldly goods rob us of our heavenly goods,
Our body rends the garment of our soul.
Our hands, as it were, prey on our feet;
Without reliance on Thee how can we live?

"God's Light"

'Tis God's Light that illumines the senses' light,
That is the meaning of "Light upon light."
The senses' light draws us earthwards.
God's Light calls us heavenwards.

"Love Casts its Own Light"

When love of God kindles a flame in the inward man,

He burns, and is freed from effects.
He has no need of signs to assure him of Love,
For Love casts its own Light up to heaven.

"The Believer's Heart"

The Prophet said that God has declared,
"I am not contained in aught above or below,
I am not contained in earth or sky, or even
In highest heaven. Know this for a surety, O beloved!
Yet am I contained in the believer's heart!
If ye seek Me, search in such hearts!"

"Self-Satisfaction"

No sickness worse than fancying thyself perfect
Can infect thy soul, O arrogant misguided one!
Shed many tears of blood from eyes and heart,
That this self-satisfaction may be driven out.
The fate of Iblis lay in saying, "I am better than He,"
And this same weakness lurks in the souls of all creatures.

"True Knowledge"

The knowledge which is not of Him is a burden;
Knowledge which comes not immediately from Him
Endures no longer than the rouge of the tire-woman.
Nevertheless, if you bear this burden in a right spirit
'Twill be removed, and you will obtain joy.
See you bear not that burden out of vainglory,
Then you will behold a store of True Knowledge within.
When you mount the steed of this True Knowledge,
Straightway the burden will fall from your back.

"The Flame of Love"

How long wilt thou dwell on words and superficialities?
A burning heart is what I want; consort with burning!
Kindle in thy heart the flame of Love,
And burn up utterly thoughts and fine expressions.
O Moses! the lovers of fair rites are one class,

They whose hearts and souls burn with Love another.

A Mother whose Children were in the Beloved's Keeping

A woman bore many children in succession, but none of them lived beyond the age of three or four months. In great distress she cried to God, and then beheld in a vision the beautiful gardens of Paradise, and many fair mansions therein, and upon one of these mansions she read her own name inscribed. And a voice from heaven informed her that God would accept the sorrows she had endured in lieu of her blood shed in holy war, as, owing to her sex, she was unable to go out to battle like the men. On looking again, the woman beheld in Paradise all the children she had lost, and she cried, "O Lord! they were lost to me, but safe with Thee!"

The Optimistic Rose

In this tale there is a warning for thee, O Soul,

That thou mayest acquiesce in God's ordinances,

And be wary and not doubt God's benevolence,

When sudden misfortune befalls thee.
Let others grow pale from fear of ill fortune,
Do thou smile like the rose at loss and gain!
For the rose, though its petals be torn asunder,
Still smiles on, and it is never cast down.

The True Mosque

Fools laud and magnify the mosque,
While they strive to oppress holy men of heart.
But the former is mere form, the latter spirit and truth.
The only true mosque is that in the hearts of saints.
The mosque that is built in the hearts of the saints
Is the place of worship of all, for God dwells there.
So long as the hearts of the saints are not afflicted,
God never destroys the nation.

"Ignorance"

Blood is impure, yet its stain is removed by water;
But that impurity of ignorance is more lasting,

Seeing that without the blessed water of God
It is not banished from the man who is subject to it.
O that thou wouldst turn thy face to thy own prayers,
And say, "Ah! my prayers are as defective as my being;
O requite me good for evil!"

A Prayer

"Pray in this wise and allay your difficulties:
'Give us good in the house of our present world,
And give us good in the house of our next world.
Make our path pleasant as a garden,
And be Thou, O Holy One, our goal!"

All Religions are One

In the adorations and benedictions of righteous men
The praises of all the prophets are kneaded together.
All their praises are mingled into one stream,

All the vessels are emptied into one ewer.

Because He that is praised is, in fact, only One.

In this respect all religions are only one religion.

Because all praises are directed towards God's Light,

These various forms and figures are borrowed from it.

A NOTE ON PERSIAN POETRY

Nizami's Discourse on Poetry

IN NIZAMI'S *The Chahãr Maqãla* ("Four Discourse"), translated by Professor Edward G. Browne, we find the *Second Discourse* devoted to "The Nature of Poetry, and the Utility of the Skilful Poet." In this interesting Discourse Nizami very amiably discusses the training required to become a poet of enduring fame, and intersperses these remarks with a number of anecdotes, which in the main are examples of the advantages derived from poetic improvisations given at opportune moments before kings when wine has gone round two or three times. Nizami sums up the nature of poetry in the following words: "Poetry is that art whereby the poet arranges imaginary propositions and adapts the deductions, with the result that he can make a little thing appear great and a great thing small, or cause good to apear in the garb of evil and evil in the garb of good." Nizami denounces the habit of giving money to old poets. He remarks: "For one so ignoble as not to have discovered in fifty years that what he writes is bad, when will he discover it?" On the other hand Nizami favours the young poet with hopeful talent, and generously remarks that "it is proper to patronise him, a duty to take care of him, and an obligation to maintain him." The minor poets of today have not these glowing advantages!

The most ingenious example of a poetic improvisation in this *Discourse* is, perhaps, one given by Rûdãgi in connection with the protracted stay of Amir Nasr bin Ahmad in Herãt. Four years the Amir camped with his army in this town, with its twenty different varieties of grape and beautiful narcissus. "He preferred Herãt to the Garden of Eden." But at length the Amir's captains and courtiers grew weary of being absent so long from Bukhãrã, where they longed to see their wives and children again. They offered Rûdãgi, the poet, five thousand dinars if he could persuade the Amir to quit Herãt and return to Bukhãrã, at an opportune moment, took up his harp and sang the following song to the Amir:

The sands of Oxus, toilsome though they be,

Beneath my feet were soft as silk to me.

Glad at the friend's return, the Oxus deep

Up to our girths in laughing waves shall leap.

Long live Bukhãrã! Be thou of good cheer!

Joyous towards thee hasteth our Amir!

The Moon's the Prince, Bukhãrã is the sky;

O sky, the Moon shall light thee by and by!

Bukhãrã the mead, the Cypress he;

Receive at last, O Mead, thy Cypress-tree!

This particular Amir seems to have been fond of flattery, and he found the daintily turned song of Rûdãgi more acceptable to his vanity than even the beauty of Herãt. He accordingly took his departure immediately the song had concluded, and, in his absent-mindedness, forgot to put on his boots, which were carried by an attendant who rode in hot pursuit.

Poetry in those days was evidently a remunerative pursuit. Nizami tells us that Khidr Khãn always had in readiness four trays of gold. "These he used to dispense by the handful" to the successful poets. Though the royal favour towards the poets was extremely bountiful, Persian poets were not always particularly courteous the one to the other. Nizami tells an amusing story of a minor poet named Rashidi. At the king's command the Poet Laureate was asked to express his opinion of Rashidi's poetry. The Poet Laureate accordingly remarked: "His verse is extremely good and chaste and correct, but it wants spice." The king afterwards repeated these words to Rashidi and bade him compose a fitting rejoinder. Rashidi composed the following verse:

You stigmatise my verse as "wanting spice,"
And possibly, my friend, you may be right.
My verse is honey-flavoured, sugar-sweet,
And spice with such could scarcely cause delight.
Spice is for you, you blackguard, not for me,
For beans and turnips is the stuff you write!

This was not kind; but Rashidi received all four baskets of gold that day!

The technical study of prosody was instituted by Khalil Ibne Ahmad-e-Bicri. He is said to have discovered this science by listening to the rhythmic beats of the fuller's mallets upon his clothes. This story is mentioned in Safi's *Treatise on Prosody.*[1] Much of Persian poetry is conventional, and the demarcation in style, due to the various phases of Persian history, is not as pronounced as might be expected. The Persian poets not only conservatively followed old metres, but old similes, old subjects as well. It was with words they were most concerned, and not with ideas. The *Lover's Companion* of Sharafu'ddin Rãmi is sufficient to prove this. This book contains a very large number of similes on the various parts of the body. This was intended to be a *vade-mecum* to the writer of erotic poetry. Professor Browne defends this conservatism and remarks that it has "guarded

1. *See The Prosody of the Persians*, by H. Blockmann, Calcutta, 1872.

the Persian language from the vulgarisation which the triumph of an untrained, untrammelled, and unconventional genius of the barbaric-degenerate type tends to produce in our own and other European tongues.

www.ingramcontent.com/pod-product-compliance
Lightning Source LLC
Chambersburg PA
CBHW062141160726
48282CB00027B/900
9789394770652